Super Veggies

Written & illustrated

By

Rhea Fenemor

DEDICATION

Dedicated to my two beautiful children who inspire me to be the best version of myself.

ACKNOWLEDGMENTS

This book wouldn't have been possible without the support, encouragement and advice of my partner, mother, brother and closest friends.
Also thank you Microsoft PowerPoint for giving me the tools needed to turn vegetables into superheroes.
And a final thank you to Kindle and Amazon to allow me to publish this book.

At the bottom of your garden, down by your feet,

live the greatest **superheroes** you will ever meet.

Orange in colour and crunchy to bite,

carrots will help with your sense of sight.

Packed with strength, energy and speed.

Potatoes will give you the power to succeed.

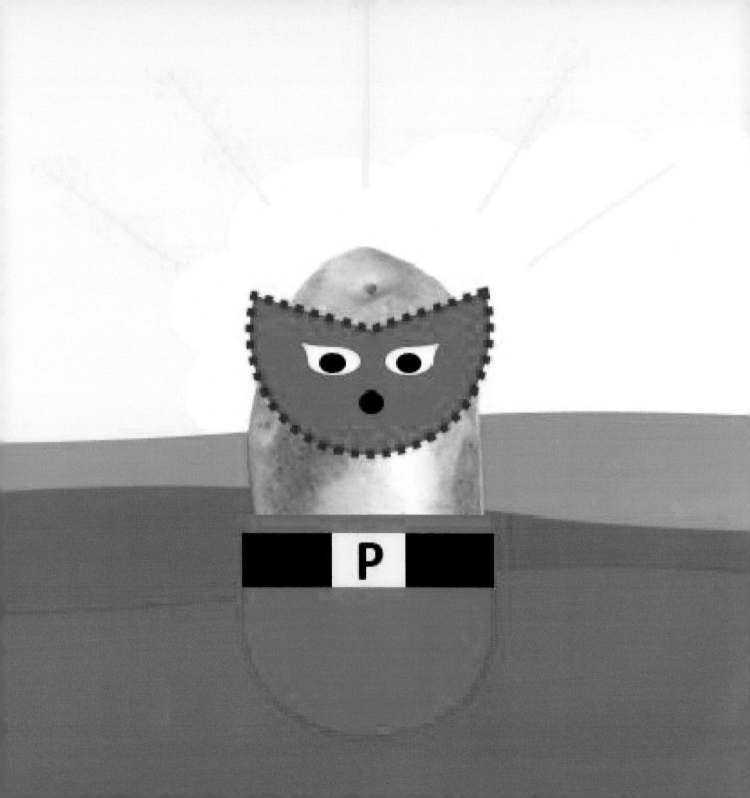

Don't turn your nose at those green little trees.

Broccoli has the power to fight disease.

Making germs shed a tear,

never fear when **onion** is here

Some foods in your tummy can cause congestion.

Vitamin packed **cabbages** will help your digestion.

And it's not just those vegetables that save the day,

fruits also have their part to play.

If you don't want no dramas,

you better eat your **bananas**.

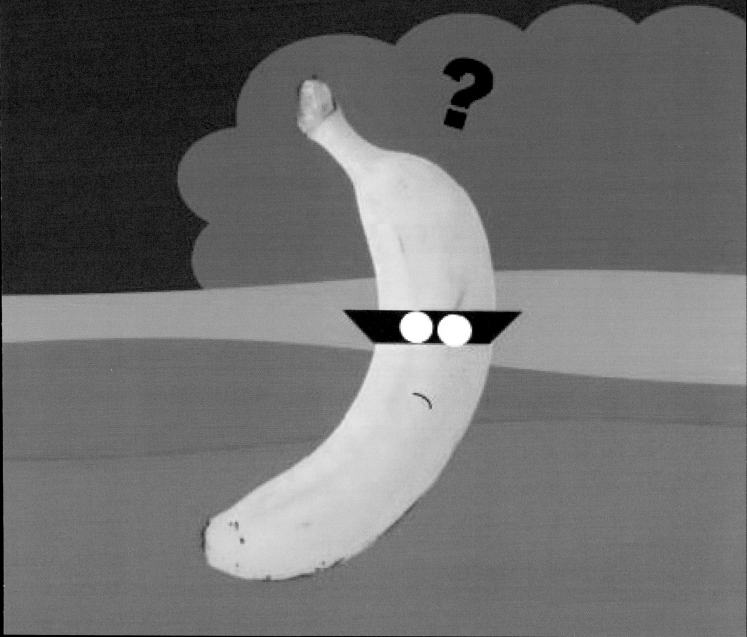

Colourful, sweet, fun and smart.

Peppers will protect your heart.

And have you heard the people say?

An **apple** a day keeps the Doctor away.

So just remember...
It is ok to eat biscuits, cakes and jellies

But if you want to grow strong,
eat fruits and veggies.

So the next time you see vegetables on your plate,
You can shout ...

"I'M SUPER! FROM THE FOODS I HAVE ATE"

The End.

Printed in Great Britain
by Amazon

62807618R00017